Play

with a purpose

with bits and pieces

BrambleKids

INTRODUCTION

YOUNG AND CREATIVE

With a focus on the world of make-believe and sharing games with siblings and friends, these activities will provide hours of concentration and entertainment.

The pleasure and pride felt from achievement, as well as the learning skills gained from completing the models, help to boost self-confidence as well as provide an ideal preparation and support for school-based learning.

NEW FROM OLD

The theme-based activities in this book afford valuable opportunities to inspire children to learn about RECYCLING. Many of the materials needed are everyday items used in the home that children can turn into something exciting!

These educational crafts will motivate children to keep and reuse many items, such as empty yoghurt pots, jars, kitchen roll tubes and newspapers. They will also teach how to correctly recycle any waste from all activities where appropriate and explain why it is important to do so.

Take Care!

Some of the activities in this book will require adult supervision. Encourage children to use scissors and pointed utensils with care and in a safe manner, further helping to build their skills and confidence.

CONTENTS

Bits and Pieces Projects

1	You will need	6–7
2	Make a Mask and Make Believe	8-9
3	Make a Sock Puppet	10
4	Make Finger Puppets and a Theatre	11
5	Make a Band	12-13
6	Make a Bell Orchestra	14
7	Make Wind Bells	15
8	Make a Sock Doll	16-17
9	Make a Robot	18
10	Make a Super Computer	19
11	Make a Mars Rover	20
12	and send it to Mars	21
13	Make a Football Game	22
14	Make a Bottle Doll	23
15	Make a Spaceman	24-25
16	Make Aliens	26
17	Make a Fern Forest	27
18	Make a Castle	28-29
19	Make a Cardboard Highway	30-31
20	Make a Snappy Crocodile	32
21	Make a Pasta Pot	33
22	Make a Fishing Game	34-35
23	Make a Balloon Person	36
24	Make your own Dough Family	37
25	Make a Seashell Paperweight and a Picture Frame	38-39
26	Make a Flock of Fluffy Sheep	40
27	Make a Spiky Porcupine	41
28	Make a Deep Sea Fish	42-43
29	Make a Dragon	44-45
30	Make Touchy-Feely Art	46-47

Development Links

Physical Skills

- **Development of fine motor skills**
  All these activities require the movement of hands and fingers. These in turn will involve the use and practice of fine motor skills and the general improvement of muscle control and strength. Developing these skills will extend into everyday activities such as washing and dressing.

- **Increase in dexterity**
  All these activities require manual dexterity. With practice and time, finer artistic skills will increase.

- **Improvements in hand-eye coordination**
  These activities require keen hand-eye coordination and such practice will support the development in further areas such as sports.

Intellectual Skills

- **Promotion of innovation and creativity**
  These activities offer children opportunities to create something new. This will encourage them to think differently and to innovate ideas.

- **Development of problem-solving skills**
  These activities require children to follow instructions and be resourceful. Encouraging them to work out where they may have gone wrong through discussion will support them in later life.

- **Enhancement of decision-making skills**
  Solving artistic challenges will promote correct and effective decision-making abilities. This will improve their ability to face other problems.

- **Improvement in memory**
  These activities require children to use and develop their visualising skills. Visualising complex designs will help improve memory.

- **Improvements in visual processing**
  These activities require children to identify patterns and colours that will naturally develop visual processing skills. This cognitive development is very important in early years.

Emotional and Social Skills

✳ Improvements in self-esteem
Encouraging children in these activities will boost their self-esteem. With each completed activity, children will feel a sense of achievement. Creating something allows children to feel in control and confident in themselves.

✳ Confident expression of self
Artistic activities encourage children to express themselves and your praise and encouragement will give them the confidence to do so. Children can channel negative and positive energy into these activities.

✳ Encouragement of creativity
Although instructed, all of the activities allow children to use their imagination and turn it into something productive. This will nurture artistic talents and self-esteem.

✳ Improvements in working with others
Encouraging children to work on these activities with their peers, whether they create a project together or simply support one another, will hugely develop their social skills and abilities. Interacting with other children with the same interests, or working together to overcome differences, will allow for friendships to develop.

✳ Strengthening of bonds
Working together with the child on these activities as a parent or teacher will strengthen your bond. Company will promote the children's enjoyment and engagement with the activity.

1 You will need

This book uses things that are usually found around the house or even things that might normally get thrown away. There are just a few things that might need to be purchased especially.

scissors

ruler

paints

string

sticky tape

paintbrushes

cardboard or kitchen roll

paper clips

balls of wool

toothpicks or cocktail sticks

needle and thread

paste

PVA

glue stick

TIP

A note about glue

There are three types of glue we have used: school glue or paste, PVA and glue sticks. If you are sticking paper and card together, then a glue stick is the best one to use. School glue is best for papier mâché and PVA is best for heavier things, hard surfaces and wool. You can also use PVA as a kind of varnish. If you paint it onto a surface, it will go shiny when it dries.

How to Make Papier Mâché

Papier mâché is a really fun material to make. It's a mix of paper and glue, or flour and water paste, which hardens when it dries. You can build up layers of paper to mould a vase or a bowl, or scrunch up torn newspaper pieces to make the shape of an animal or person.

Papier mâché takes a long time to dry, so wait before you paint or decorate it.

Things to Remember

If you are covering an object to make a papier-mâché mould, it's best to cover the object in cling film to start with. Use school glue or flour mixed with water into a thick paste. The more layers you add, the firmer your shape will be. Make sure the paper is really soggy with paste for the best results. It won't be waterproof.

- sticks or twigs
- balloons
- coloured paper
- nuts and bolts
- peg
- seeds and rice
- bowl and old spoon
- plaster powder

2 Make a Mask

It's fun to pretend you are someone you are not.
Or to hide behind a mask and become a fierce animal.

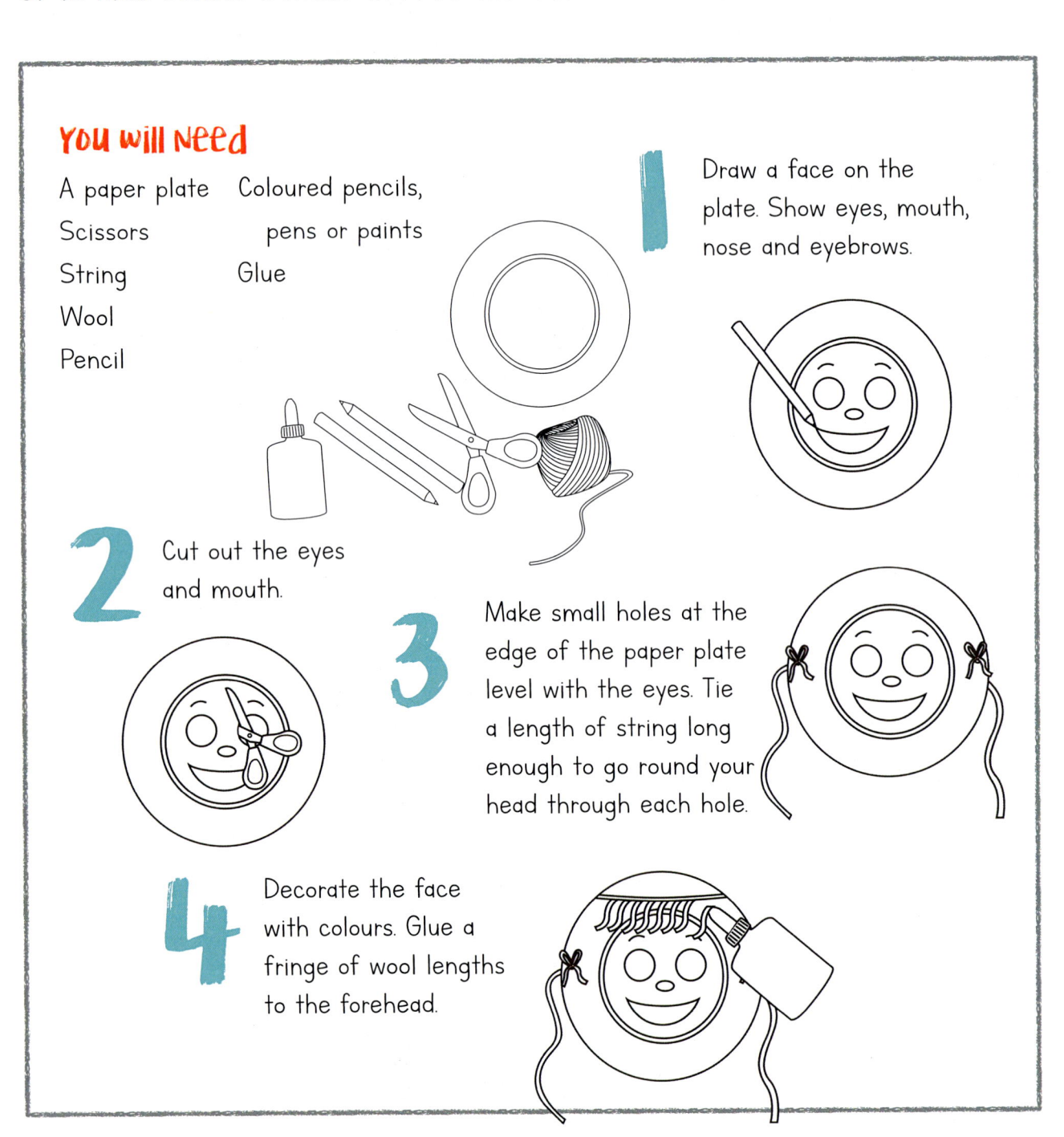

You will need

A paper plate
Scissors
String
Wool
Pencil

Coloured pencils, pens or paints
Glue

1 Draw a face on the plate. Show eyes, mouth, nose and eyebrows.

2 Cut out the eyes and mouth.

3 Make small holes at the edge of the paper plate level with the eyes. Tie a length of string long enough to go round your head through each hole.

4 Decorate the face with colours. Glue a fringe of wool lengths to the forehead.

8

5 Tie the mask over your ears so that it doesn't slip down.

Make believe

Dressing up in a few old or interesting clothes can be fun.

A dressing-up box filled with hats, clothes, beads, beards and feathers can change you into a crowd of different characters.

3 Make a sock puppet

You will need
An old white sock   Coloured felt-tip pens

1 Pull the sock over the hand you don't write with. Clench your fist, tucking any spare sock under your fingers.

2 Using a felt-tip pen, draw a face onto the sock. Make this the face of any animal or insect you like. You might want to make up a monster face or something as extraordinary.

The mouth will work best if it is drawn on a line with the top of your thumb.

Draw the eyes on the knuckles of your first finger.

3 Practice making the face move into different expressions.

And invent a way that your puppet speaks.

TIP If you make two puppets, you could put on a talking puppet show.

4 Make Finger Puppets

You will need

Felt-tip pens   Wool   Scissors
Small box   Washable glue

1 Draw faces on the tips of your first and second fingers. Make them funny. Perhaps include a really happy face and a really sad one.

2 Glue, or tie, short lengths of wool to your puppet heads as hair, or even make some of them a paper hat.

...and a Theatre

3 For the theatre, remove one side of the box and cut two holes in the top so you can poke your fingers up through it and wiggle them about.

Decorate the box.

5 Make a band

Get together with a few friends and form a band. You will need to make your own instruments using these ideas.

1 A jam jar xylophone

You can make all kinds of different sounds from jam jars filled with water. Fill the jars with different amounts of water and tap the side gently with a wooden spoon to make a sound. Try to make a scale, if you can.

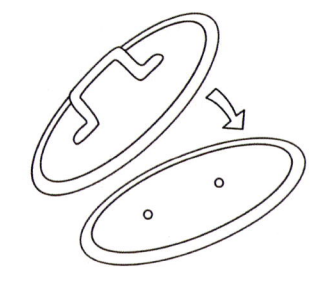

2 Maracas

Put a little rice or a few dried peas into an empty washing-up liquid bottle. Push the top back on tightly or close the opening with sticky tape. Shake the bottle to a rhythm and beat.

3 Tin drum

Stretch a rubber band around an empty cocoa tin. You don't need the lid on. Now pluck the rubber band where it is stretched over the open end of the tin to make a plonking beat.

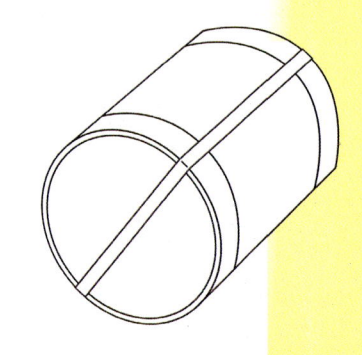

4 Cymbals

Clash two metal saucepan lids together to make an odd loud clang.

5 Castanets

Knock wooden or metal spoons together.

And lastly – you!

Use your voice to make hissing, gurgling, wheezing and grinding sounds. Join in with other body noises. Clap your hands, click your fingers, slap your thighs and stamp your feet.

6 Guitar

Stretch rubber bands of different thicknesses over a metal roasting tray.

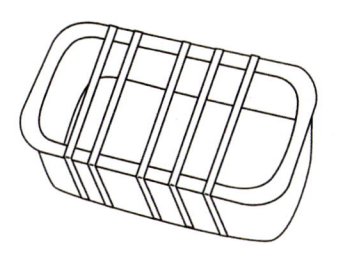

TIP If you can record your band, add breathing sounds into the microphone, or sprinkle grains of rice near to it for a pattering effect.

6 Make a bell orchestra

You can play tunes on your own bell orchestra.

You will need
Several clean terracotta flowerpots – not plastic
A ball of string
A broomstick or long rod
Sticky tape
Thickly mixed paints
A paintbrush
A wooden spoon

1 Paint patterns on the flowerpots.

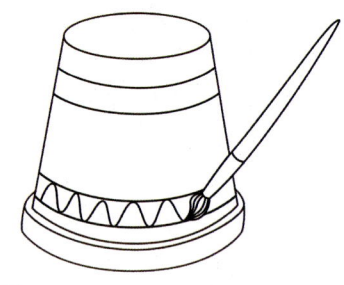

2 Cut one length of string for each flowerpot. The shortest should be about 20 centimetres long. Each length should be a little longer than the previous one.

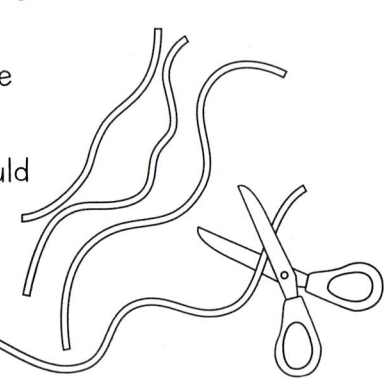

3 Knot each length of string around the rod making sure they are some distance from each other. Make sure they stay in place using sticky tape.

4 Thread the loose ends of the string through the hole in the top of each flowerpot and tie them firmly with a large knot. The knot must be larger than the hole.

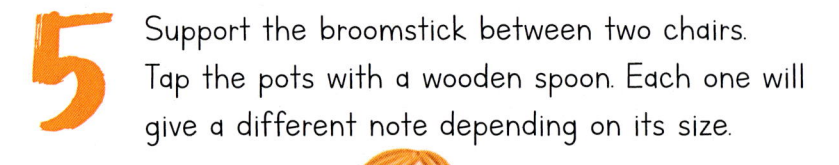

5 Support the broomstick between two chairs. Tap the pots with a wooden spoon. Each one will give a different note depending on its size.

7 Make wind bells

In some countries, lightweight bells are hung up for decoration. They make a gentle tinkling sound as the breeze moves them.

You will need

Clean foil carton tops or circles of kitchen foil
Lemon squeezer or some household object with a cone-shaped top
Small beads
Scissors
Needle and thread
2 twigs

1 Cut out foil circles of different sizes. Press them over the lemon squeezer to make their shape. Remove them carefully.

2 Cut out small heart shapes from the foil.

3 Thread a needle and tie a knot in the end. Sew through the top of the heart.

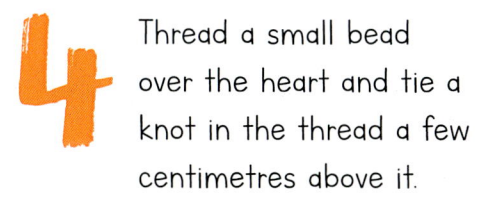

4 Thread a small bead over the heart and tie a knot in the thread a few centimetres above it.

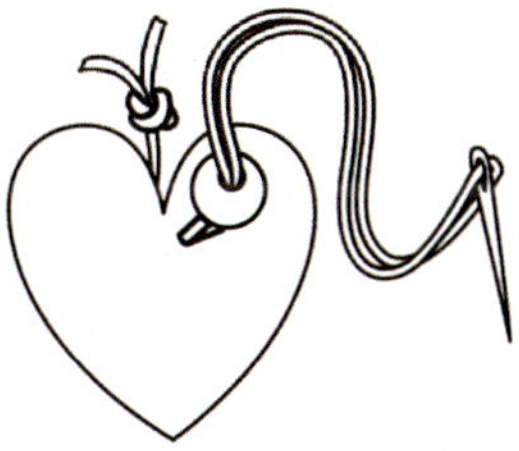

5 Stitch though the centre of the bell and add another bead. Make more bells like this.

6 Bind the twigs together to make a cross piece and hang your bells from it.

8 Make a sock doll

You will need

Five old socks –
　　three short ones
　　and two long ones
Cotton wool
String
Needle
Strong thread

1 Fill two of the short socks with cotton wool in a sausage shape and firmly tie the ends with string.

2 Fill the other short sock with lots of cotton wool to make a ball shape. Tie the end again.

3 Start filling one of the long socks with cotton wool in a sausage shape. When you get half way, tie some string around the middle and then carry on. Fill up the other half and then tie it up with string once more.

4 Take the last long sock and fill it with cotton wool in a ball shape.

5 Now you have a head, a body, two arms and two legs. Sew them all together.

6 If you are good at sewing, you could sew on some hair and a face, or you could draw a face on paper, cut it out and stick it on with glue.

17

9 Make a Robot

You will need

- Paintbrush
- Scissors
- PVA glue
- Piece of card
- Silver paint
- Cardboard tube from kitchen roll or toilet paper
- Small lid
- Tin foil
- Bendy wire
- Nuts and bolts to decorate

1 Ask an adult to help you cut three panels out of the side of the cardboard roll. Glue shiny paper over these 'windows'.

2 Paint the rest of the roll with silver paint or wrap it in silver foil.

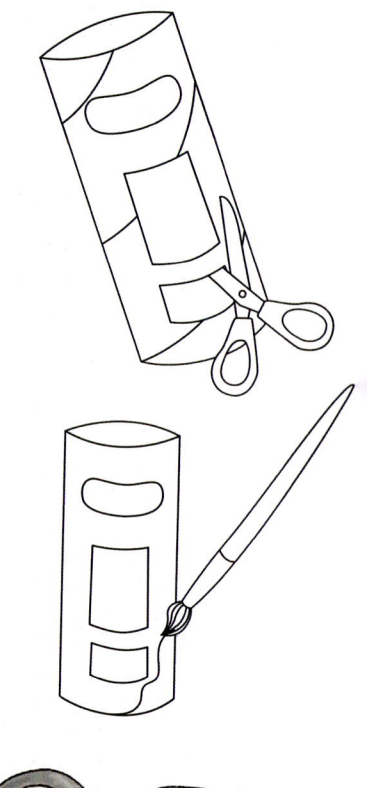

3 Stick on lots of different nuts and bolts, knobs and dials all over the body of your robot.

4 Glue bolts or curtain rings onto the small lid to make eyes. Then glue the lid onto the top of the robot's body.

5 Cut out card circles and paint them silver. Thread them onto the thin wire and poke them through the card to make moveable arms.

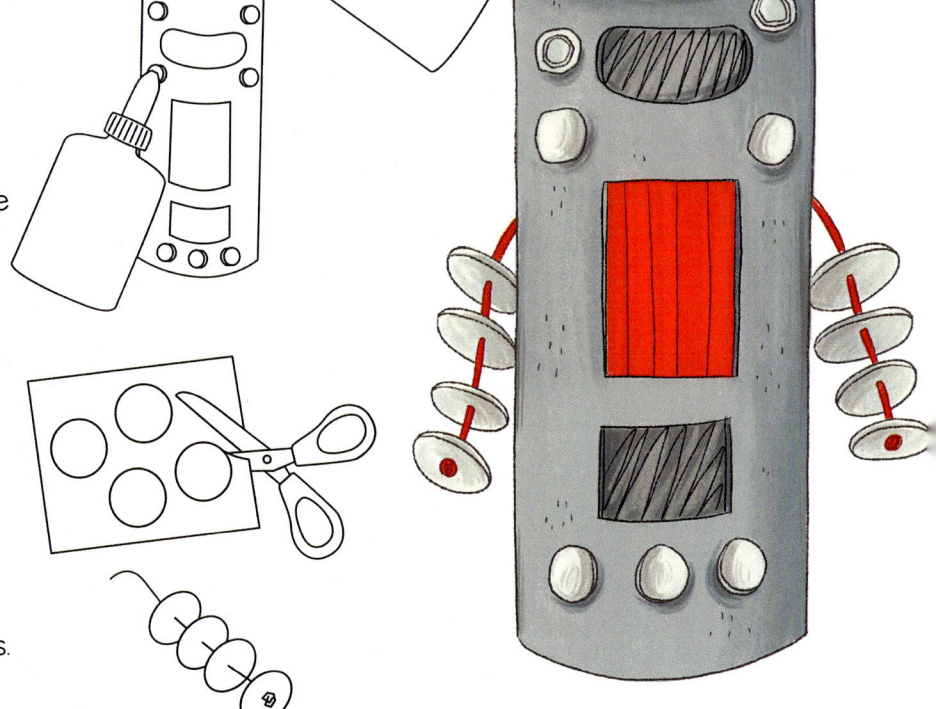

10 Make a Super Computer

Computers are getting smaller and smaller, but a "super computer" is a very powerful, huge machine used by scientists and engineers.

You will need

Lots of boxes and tubes of different shapes and sizes
Cardboard scraps
Paper
Paintbrush
PVA glue
Silver and other coloured paints
Felt-tip pens
Scissors

Use all the bits and pieces you can find to build this amazing model. Each piece can have its own special look and identity.

Cover the units with dials, clocks, gauges and instructions. Cut out paper discs and mark them with figures. Glue them all over your machine.

11 Make a Mars Rover ...

It takes a special kind of car to travel on the Moon or on one of the planets. But a rover named Perseverance has landed on Mars.

You will need
- A number of small cardboard boxes of different sizes
- Card
- Toothpicks
- Pencil
- Glue
- Kitchen foil
- Coloured paints and brushes

1 Glue the boxes together to make a shape like this.

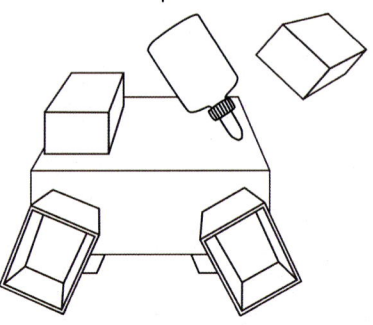

2 Roll and glue strips of card into cylinders for the legs. Glue these onto the body of the rover.

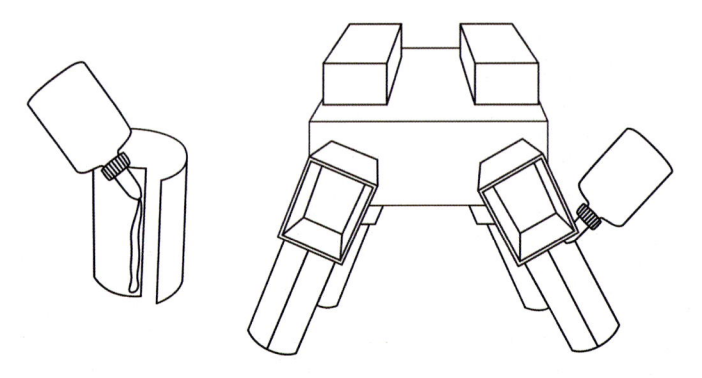

3 Draw and then cut out a circle from the card. Cut a straight line from the centre to the edge of the circle.

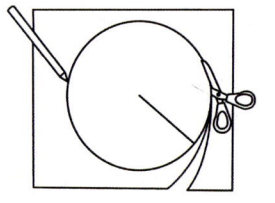

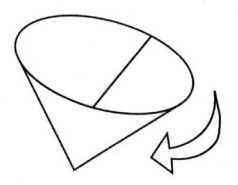

Fold and glue the circle to make a cone shape. This makes the satellite probe. Glue it to the top of one of the boxes.

4 Glue the toothpicks together to make an antenna and fix this to the rover too.

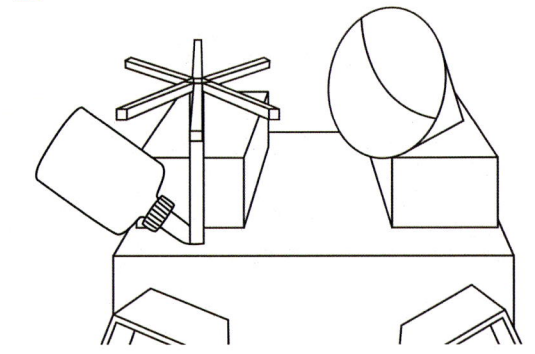

20

5 Paint the vehicle and decorate it with shiny kitchen foil.

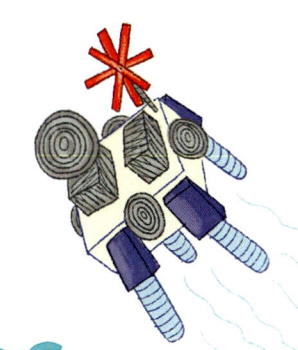

12 ... and send it to Mars

You will need

Papier-mâché paste made from torn pieces of newspaper mixed with thin paste
A strong board for the base
Paintbrushes and paints

Using your hands and fingers to shape the papier mâché into a Mars landscape on the board.

Use your fingers to press out craters and to mound high mountains and ridges.

Leave to dry before painting the landscape with orangey-red paints.

And position your rover on the ground.

13 Make a Football Game

You will need

A shallow cardboard box
Green paper
White paint
Brush
Saucer to draw round
Ruler
Small paper cups
Scissors
Glue
Toothpicks
Tape
A small ball
Paper drinking straws

1 Cut the green paper so that it will fit neatly inside the box. Use the white paint to draw the lines on the pitch.

2 Draw round the paper cup in the middle, and then use the saucer to make two semicircles at each end. Paint the straight lines by using the ruler.

3 Cut a paper cup in half and stick one half at each end of the pitch to make a goal. Leave it to dry.

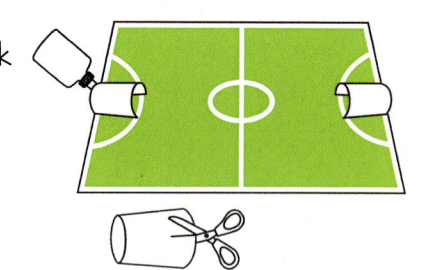

4 Make four flags for each corner by taping some coloured paper to toothpicks. Make them stand up in the corners of the box.

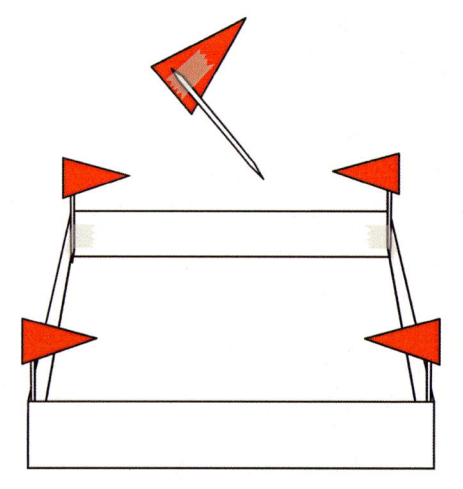

Put the paper inside the box and you are ready to play with a friend.

22

14 Make a bottle doll

You will need
A clean empty bottle
Kitchen roll tube
Scissors
Scraps of material
Coloured paper
Paint
Brush

1 Draw a face onto the kitchen roll tube and put it over the neck of the bottle.

2 Make some clothes out of paper or material and stick them on.

5 Get two straws and a light ball. If you don't have a ball, you can use a small piece of paper or tin foil scrunched up tightly. Take up position at either end of the pitch and blow down the straws behind the ball to push it into the goal.

15 Make a Spaceman

You will need

Tins of different sizes.**
**THESE SHOULD BE CLEAN AND WITH NO SHARP EDGES WHERE THE LIDS HAVE BEEN REMOVED. ASK AN ADULT TO HELP YOU.
PVA glue
Tin foil
Grey paint made my mixing black and white paints
Brush
Felt-tip pens

1 Stick the tins together with the glue. This will take a little time to set.

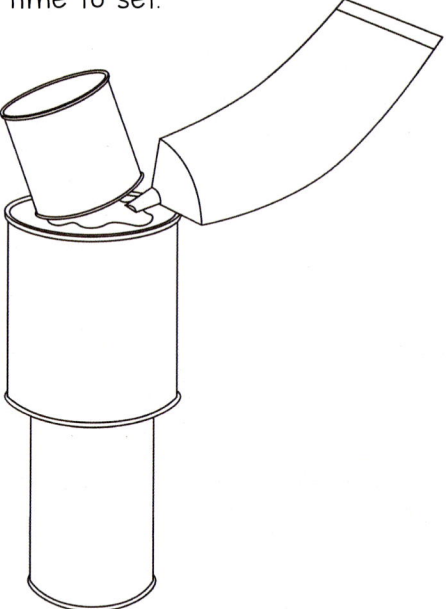

2 Paint them light grey with thick paint.

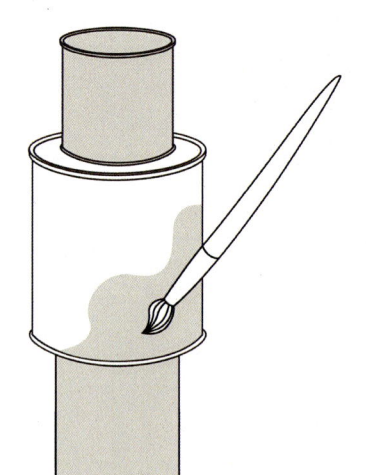

3 Make some hands and feet out of the tin foil and stick them on.

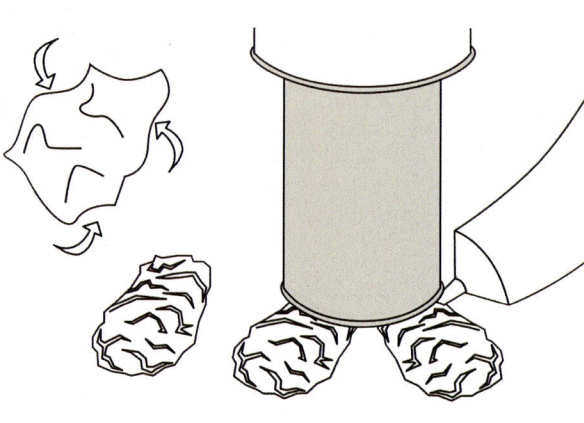

4 When everything is dry, draw on lots of details with the pens.

25

16 Make aliens

You will need
Coloured modelling clay

1 Break off bits of clay and roll them around in your hands until they are soft and easy to use.

2 Roll the clay into sausage shapes and balls.

3 Make aliens with funny and unusual bodies.

You can have lots of fun making different aliens. And you never know but one of them may be just like the real thing!

17 Make a Fern Forest

You will need
Fern leaves
Paints
Paint brush
White and black cardboard

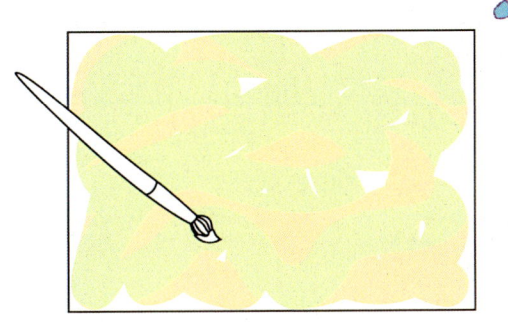

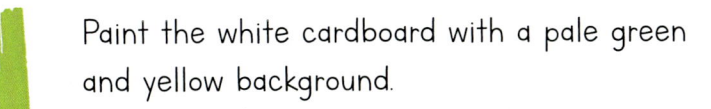

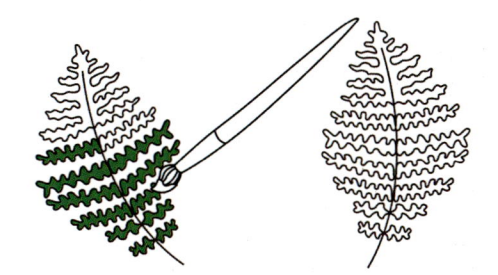

1. Paint the white cardboard with a pale green and yellow background.

2. Paint the leaves with dark green, and other dark colours that you like.

3. Place the painted ferns face down on the background. Put a piece of paper over the top and gently rub over the leaves to get a good print.

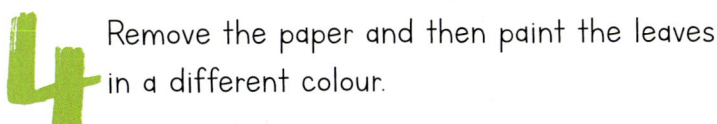

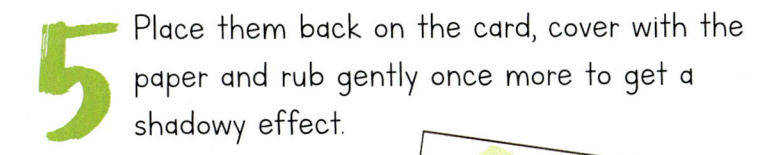

4. Remove the paper and then paint the leaves in a different colour.

5. Place them back on the card, cover with the paper and rub gently once more to get a shadowy effect.

18 Make a Castle

You will need

A cardboard box
Four kitchen roll tubes
Paint
Brush
Scissors
PVA glue
String
Tape
Toothpicks
Paper
Newspaper

1 Cut out small squares all along the top of the box and the cardboard tubes to form battlements.

2 Stick the kitchen roll tubes to each corner of the box for the turrets.

3 Cut a door for the castle but leave it attached at the bottom so that it flaps down.

4 When the glue has dried, you can paint your castle. Let the first layer of paint dry and then add windows and a stone pattern.

5 Draw two flags on the paper and cut them out. Tape them to the toothpicks and stick them in the turrets.

6 To make the door go up and down, pull down the door and tape a piece of string to each side.

Measure the string up to the top of the door. Make two holes on either side. Pass the string through and tie a knot. Now when you pull the string, the door will go up.

To Make a Base for the Castle

Place your castle in the middle of a large square of cardboard. Draw a wavy line around the castle to form the moat. Scrunch up the newspaper and stick on the card. When it is dry, paint it green for the grass and blue for the moat.

19 Make a cardboard highway

You will need

A large piece of thick card
Newspaper
Scissors
Pens
Glue
Paints
Brush
Toothpicks
Clear plastic bottle
Thin card
Modelling clay
Tape

1 Draw the outline of a road on the large piece of thick card.

2 Scrunch up the newspaper and glue it onto the card in the gaps between the road.

3 Cut the plastic bottle in half and then cut off both ends. Glue it onto the road to make a tunnel.

4 Cut a piece of thin card and glue it over the tunnel to make a bridge.

5 Let all the glue dry and then paint the road grey and the hills green.

6 When the grey paint is dry you can paint the lines on the road. Don't forget a stripy crossing.

Draw some road signs, trees and traffic lights onto the thin card.

Cut them out and tape them onto the toothpicks.

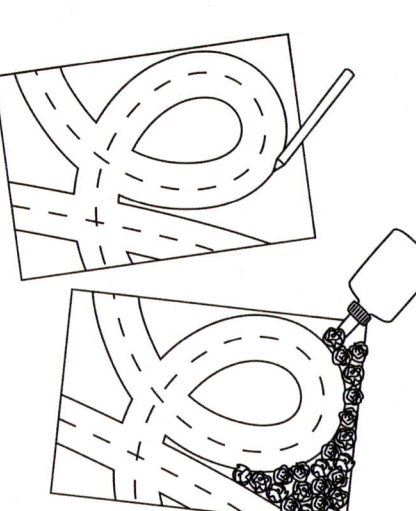

TiP Stick the road signs and other bits into small lumps of modelling clay so that they stand up. Arrange them on your road system. You can also add some cardboard buildings if you have space.

20 Make a Snappy Crocodile

You will need
Wooden pegs
Paper
Glue
Scissors
Felt-tip pens

1 Draw a small crocodile on the paper, about the size of the peg. Colour it with a scaly crocodile skin using the felt-tip pens.

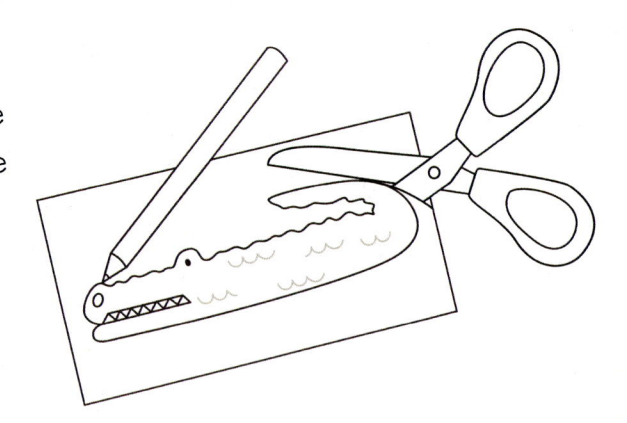

2 Carefully cut it out and then cut in half lengthwise.

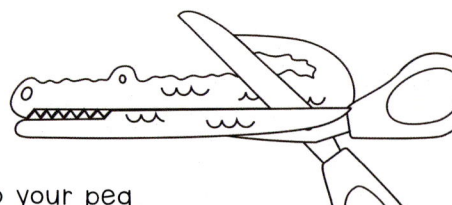

3 Glue both halves onto your peg so that the mouth is together.

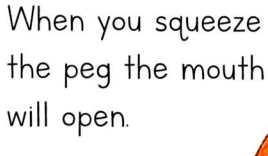

When you squeeze the peg the mouth will open.

21 Make a Pasta Pot

You will need
A cup
Cling film
PVA glue
Pasta or noodles of different shapes

1 Turn the cup upside down and cover it with cling film.

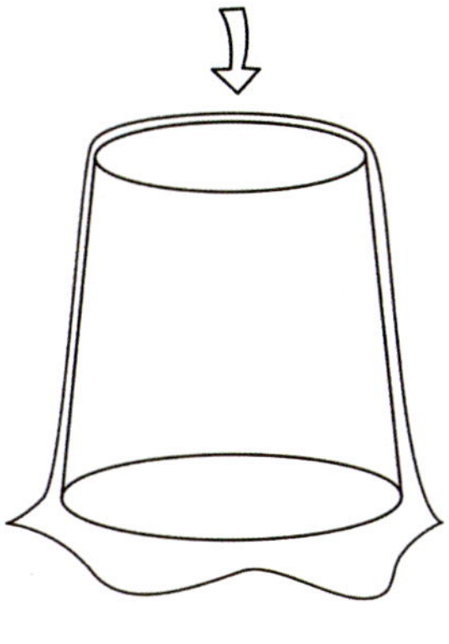

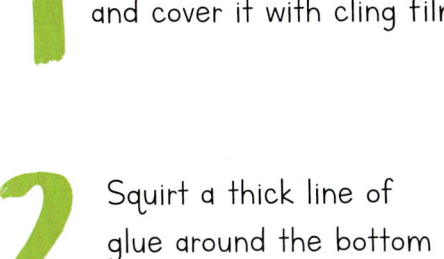

2 Squirt a thick line of glue around the bottom and start sticking the pasta neatly to the glue.

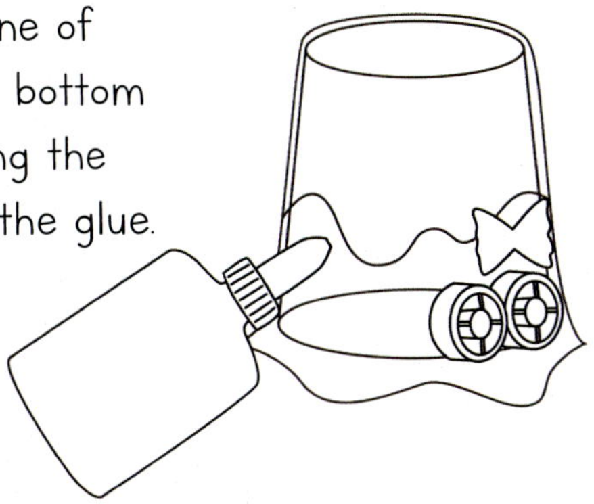

3 Squirt another layer of glue above the first one and stick on more pasta. Push down well so that it fits well into the first row and so that the glue oozes out.

Keep going until you've covered the cup. Then leave it to dry.

4 Gently take if off the cup, and remove the cling film.

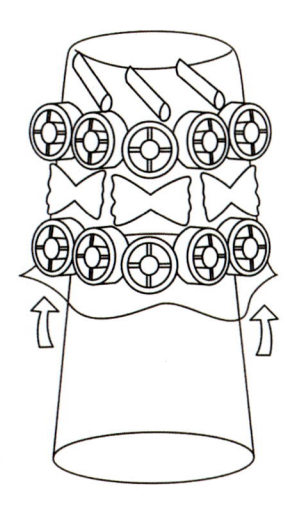

Tip If you have a small torch, put it inside so that the light can shine through.

22 Make a Fishing Game

You will need

A shallow box
Blue tissue paper
Glue
Stiff card
Paper clips
String
Paper drinking straws

First make the pond by decorating the box.

1 Rip up the blue tissue paper and glue it all over the box.

2 Make the base a little uneven by scrunching up some tissue and gluing it on.

3 Cut lots of fish out of the card and colour them in.

4 Fix a paper clip to the mouth of each fish, but don't push it all the way down. Leave a loop at the end.

5 Tie some string to the straws.

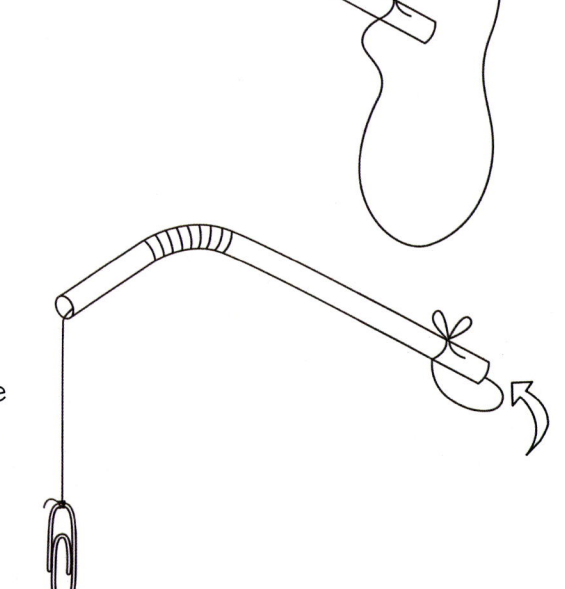

6 Tie a paper clip onto the bottom and pull out the end to make a hook.

7 Put the fish in the pond and start fishing!

TIP This is a great game to play with your friends. Who can catch the most fish?

23 Make a balloon person

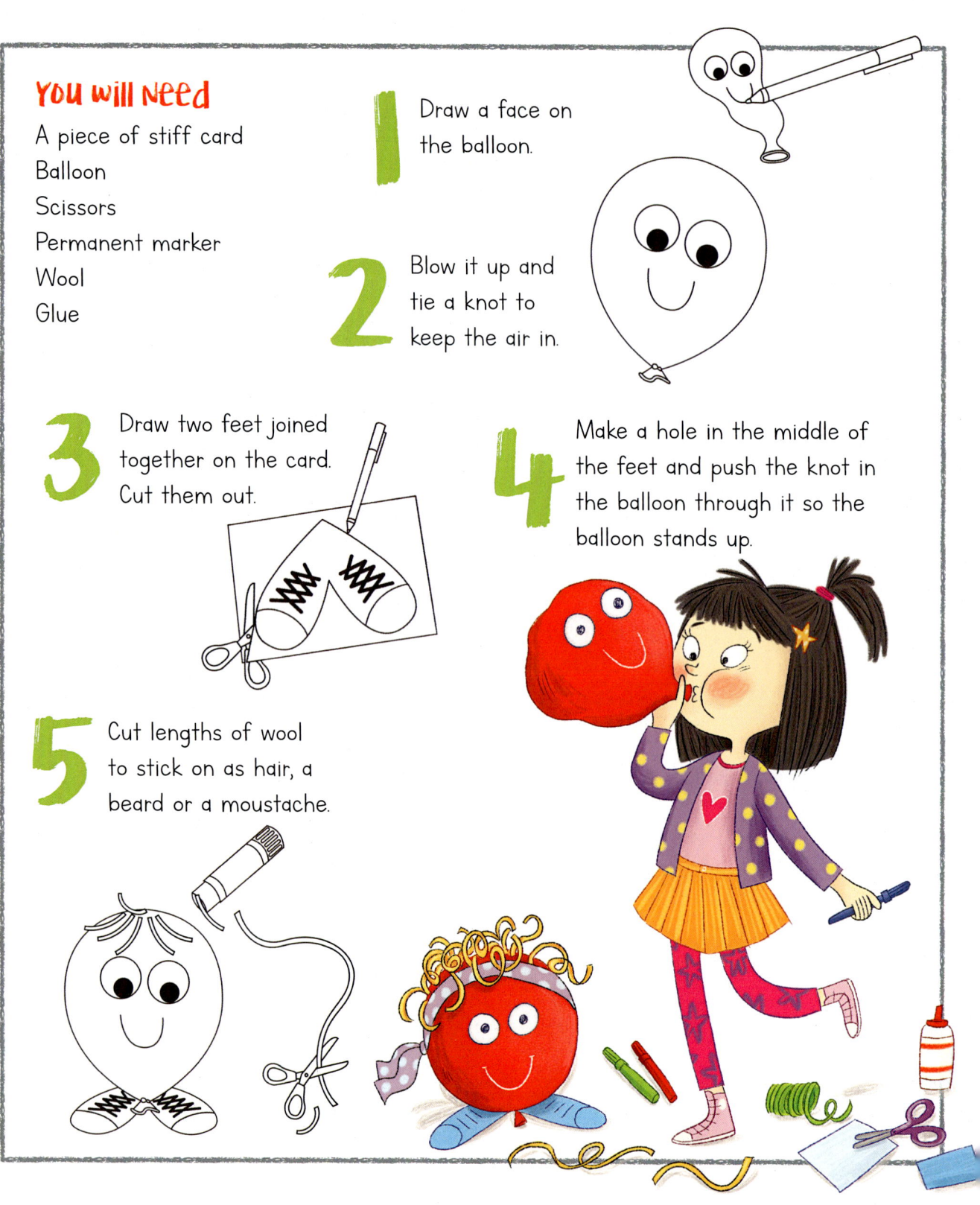

You will need

A piece of stiff card
Balloon
Scissors
Permanent marker
Wool
Glue

1 Draw a face on the balloon.

2 Blow it up and tie a knot to keep the air in.

3 Draw two feet joined together on the card. Cut them out.

4 Make a hole in the middle of the feet and push the knot in the balloon through it so the balloon stands up.

5 Cut lengths of wool to stick on as hair, a beard or a moustache.

24 Make your own dough family

You will need
250 grammes flour
Warm water
Tablespoon of salt
Tablespoon of vegetable oil
Paint
A bowl for mixing
Spoon
Rolling pin

Make the dough
Put the flour, oil and salt into the bowl.
Mix them together well.
Start adding the water a little at a time.
Stir it well each time you add some.
When the mixture feels stiff, form it into a ball with your hands and knead it together into a smooth dough.
(If it's too sticky, add some more flour.
If it's too dry, add a tiny bit more water.)

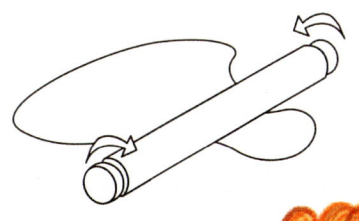

Make the family
You can use the dough to make flat or round shapes. Roll it out with a rolling pin and cut out shapes to make all the members of your family. Paint them when the dough is dry.

You can also make animals that stand up by sticking balls together.

25 Make a Seashell Paperweight

You will need

Plaster powder
A bowl for mixing
A large smooth, rounded stone
Odds and ends to decorate the paperweight such as shells, small stones, beads and sequins
Paints
Brush
Spoon

1 Mix the plaster with water to make a thick paste.

Spread it thickly over the stone.

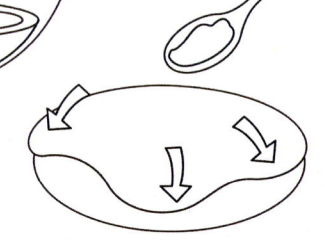

2 Press your shells, stones and beads into the plaster to form a pattern.

TIP Don't worry if you don't get it right the first time. Just smooth if off and start again.

3 When it's dry you can paint it.

4 If you have an old picture frame that nobody wants, you can decorate it in the same way.

and a picture frame

26 Make a flock of fluffy sheep

You will need
Different sorts of textured paper
White card
Cotton wool
Scissors
Pens
Glue
Paint
Brush

1 Draw a few sheep onto a piece of card and cut them out.

2 Colour in the legs and heads.

3 Glue small clumps of cotton wool onto the bodies.

4 Make a patchwork field by sticking squares of textured paper onto another piece of card.

Paint the squares green and brown.

5 When the field is dry, glue on the sheep.

27 Make a Spiky Porcupine

You will need
Modelling clay
Beads
Toothpicks
Leaves in a box.

1 Roll the clay into a ball.

2 Pinch one end to make the nose.

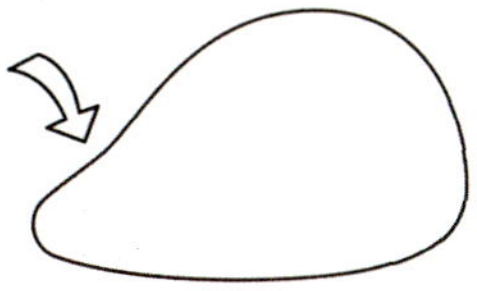

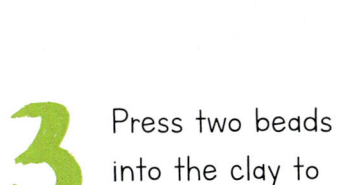

3 Press two beads into the clay to make eyes.

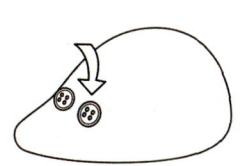

4 Scratch some fur onto the face with a toothpick.

5 Stick lots of toothpicks into the clay all over the body.

6 Place it in the leafy nest.

41

28 Make a deep sea fish

You will need

An old sock
Newspaper
Coloured paper
PVA glue
Bottle tops
Scissors
Sand or salt
String
Paints
Brush
A bowl for mixing

1 Fill the sock with scrunched up newspaper. Tie the end of the sock to close it.

2 Take some of the coloured paper, fold it in half and cut out a zigzag to make the back fin.

3 Fold some more coloured paper back and forth to make a fan.

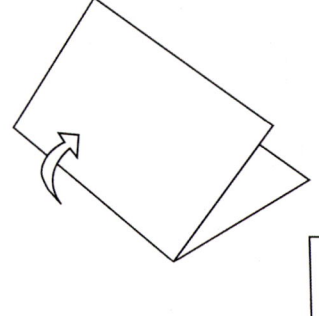

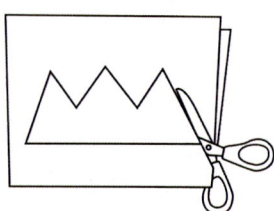

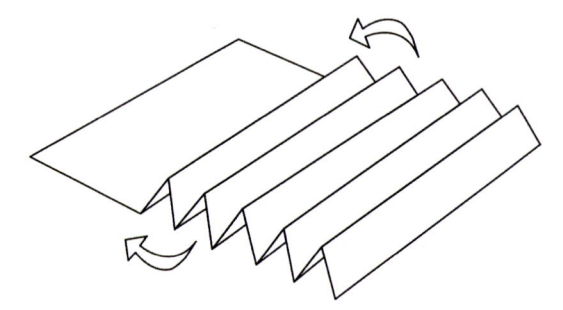

4 Cut it into two small fins and a tail.

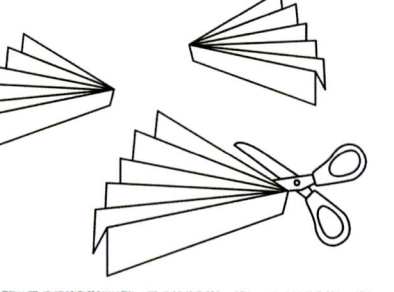

4 Stick all the parts, including the bottle tops for eyes, onto your fish. Use lots of glue. Leave it to dry.

5 Mix together the sand, or salt, some glue and some paint. Paint all over the fish to give your deep sea monster a rough and scaly skin.

29 Make a dragon

You will need
Coloured paper
Two sticks
Pens
Glue
Tape
Red and orange tissue paper

1 Cut two long strips of different coloured paper and stick them together to form an L shape.

2 Fold the first colour over the second colour and then the second colour over the first.

Keep going until you run out of paper. Glue it together to make a concertina.

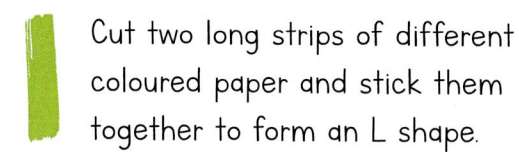

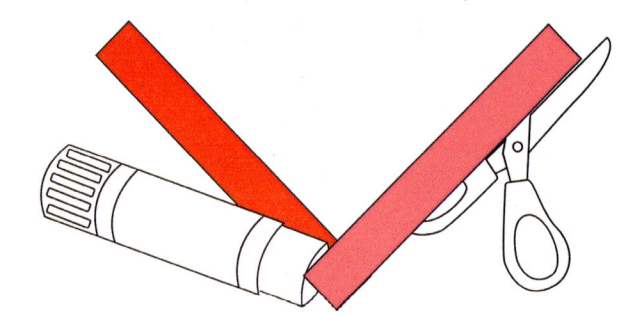

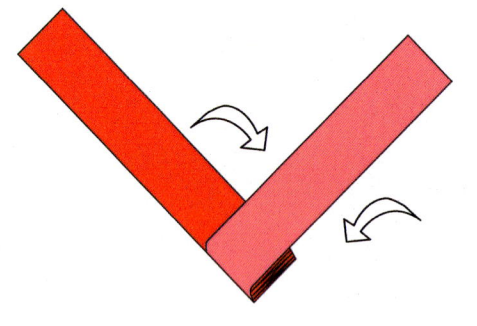

3 Glue some bits of tissue onto a piece of coloured paper to make flames.

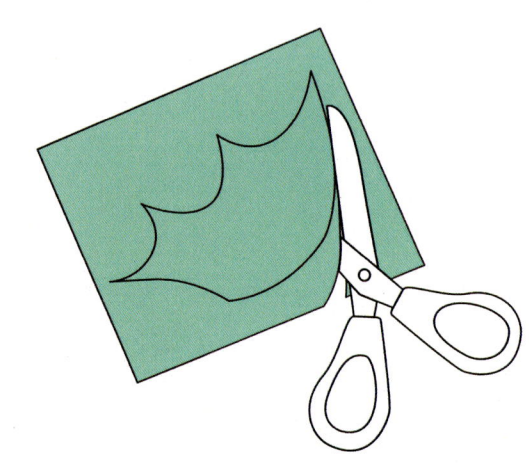

Roll it up and fix it with tape. Stick it to your concertina.

4 Cut out some wing shapes and stick them to the side of your concertina.

5 Tape two sticks to each end and make your dragon dance.

45

30 Make Touchy-Feely Art

How something feels is called its texture. You can have lots of fun exploring how things feel. Try putting some things in a box and asking your friend to guess what they are, just by feeling them.

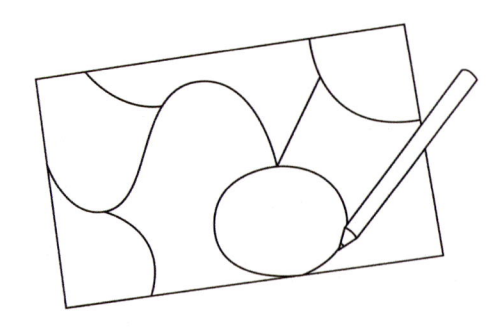

You will need

A big piece of cardboard
PVA glue
Scissors
Pencil
Foil
Tissue paper
Cotton wool
Sand
String
Dried grass
Small pebbles
Sponge
Any other things you can find around the house that have an interesting texture.

1 Draw a pattern on the card.

2 Use all the things you have collected to make lots of different textures. Scrunch and rip up paper, roll up string and cut up the sponge.

3 Glue them all onto the cardboard, filling the parts of your pattern.

4 When your art is dry, close your eyes and gently rub your hand over the picture. See if you can remember all the different things you stuck on. You can ask your friends to guess too.

WRITTEN BY: FELICIA LAW with additional material from LUCY BRIGNALL

EDUCATIONAL TEXT: AIMÉE JACKSON

DESIGN: FELICIA LAW: IMRAN KELLY

COLOUR ILLUSTRATIONS: ELISA ROCCHI (BEEHIVE ILLUSTRATION AGENCY)

BLACK LINE ILLUSTRATIONS: KERI GREEN (BEEHIVE ILLUSTRATION AGENCY)

P6-7 ART - MARTINA ROTONDO

COPYRIGHT © 2021 BrambleKids Ltd

ISBN: 978-1-914411-50-2